THE PENGUIN POETS

U. A. FANTHORPE

SELECTED POEMS

U. A. Fanthorpe was born in Kent in 1929 and educated at Oxford. Until she became a 'middle-aged drop-out' and began working as a clerk in a Bristol hospital, she taught at Cheltenham for many years. In 1980 she won third prize in the massive *Observer/Arvon/South Bank Show* poetry competition and she was awarded one of the two £1,000 Travelling Scholarships for 1983 by The Society of Authors. Between 1983 and 1985 she held an Arts Council Writer's Fellowship at St Martin's College, Lancaster. In 1987 she was awarded a Hawthornden Scholarship, and was the 1987–88 Northern Arts Fellow at the universities of Durham and Newcastle upon Tyne.

Her first volume of poems, *Side Effects* (Peterloo Poets, 1978), received extraordinary critical acclaim. Charles Causley, writing in *Arts South West*, called her 'a new and original voice in English poetry: clear, distinctive, and remarkably assured' and welcomed her volume as 'the most accomplished first book of poems I have come across in several years'. Her second volume, *Standing To* (Peterloo Poets, 1982), was chosen 'My Book of the Year' by Robin Lane Fox, poetry reviewer for the *Financial Times*, 'because this second collection has an assurance, wit, and sense of pathos which excel anything I have found in this year's imaginative literature'. In his review of the volume in the same paper he declared: 'Who, though, will move you, going straight for the emotions? Unhesitatingly, I name U. A. Fanthorpe as the poet who can suddenly hit you below the heart.' U. A. Fanthorpe's third volume, *Voices Off* (Peterloo Poets, 1984), was welcomed by Sarah Peel in *City Limits* as 'poetry of intuitive intelligence: a massive achievement'. *A Watching Brief* (Peterloo Poets, 1987), *Neck Verse* (Peterloo Poets, 1992) and *Safe as Houses* (1995) have attracted widespread critical acclaim, and she has recently contributed a selection of poems to *Penguin Modern Poets: Volume 6*. Her originality in voice and subject matter has been highlighted by George Szirtes writing in *The Times Literary Supplement*: 'Her poems are particularly good when they offer unaffected voices from a gallery of human types that do not usually figure in poetry ... They speak an often humorous, often painful stoic

wisdom.' This collection includes poems from her first three Peterloo volumes and was a 1986 *Sunday Telegraph* 'Book of the Year' choice.

U. A. Fanthorpe is a Fellow of the Royal Society of Literature. She lives in Gloucestershire.

Double Act, a Penguin Audiobook of U. A. Fanthorpe's poetry, is also available.

U. A. FANTHORPE

SELECTED POEMS

PENGUIN BOOKS

PENGUIN BOOKS

Published by the Penguin Group
Penguin Books Ltd, 27 Wrights Lane, London W8 5TZ, England
Penguin Putnam Inc., 375 Hudson Street, New York, New York 10014, USA
Penguin Books Australia Ltd, Ringwood, Victoria, Australia
Penguin Books Canada Ltd, 10 Alcorn Avenue, Toronto, Ontario, Canada M4V 3B2
Penguin Books (NZ) Ltd, Private Bag 102902, NSMC, Auckland, New Zealand

Penguin Books Ltd, Registered Offices: Harmondsworth, Middlesex, England

Side Effects first published by Peterloo Poets 1978
Standing To first published by Peterloo Poets 1982
Voices Off first published by Peterloo Poets 1984
This selection first published by Peterloo Poets 1986
Published in Penguin Books 1986
11 13 15 17 19 20 18 16 14 12

Printed in England by Clays Ltd, St Ives plc
Photoset in 10/11 pt Linotron Ehrhardt

FOR ROSEMARIE BAILEY

Contents

FROM *Voices Off*

FROM *Side Effects*

The List

Flawlessly typed, and spaced
At the proper intervals,
Serene and lordly, they pace
Along tomorrow's list
Like giftbearers on a frieze.

In tranquil order, arrayed
With the basic human equipment –
A name, a time, a number –
They advance on the future.

Not more harmonious who pace
Holding a hawk, a fish, a jar
(The customary offerings)
Along the Valley of the Kings.

Tomorrow these names will turn nasty,
Senile, pregnant, late,
Handicapped, handcuffed, unhandy,
Muddled, moribund, mute,

Be stained by living. But here,
Orderly, equal, right,
On the edge of tomorrow, they pause
Like giftbearers on a frieze

With the proper offering,
A time, a number, a name.
I am the artist, the typist;
I did my best for them.

For Saint Peter

I have a good deal of sympathy for you, mate,
Because I reckon that, like me, you deal with the outpatients.

Now the inpatients are easy, they're cowed by the nurses
(In your case, the angels) and they know what's what in the set-up.

They know about God (in my case Dr Snow) and all His little
    fads,
And if there's any trouble with them, you can easily scare them
    rigid

Just by mentioning His name. But outpatients are different.
They bring their kids with them, for one thing, and that creates a
    wrong atmosphere.

They have shopping baskets, and buses to catch. They cry, or knit,
Or fall on the floor in convulsions. In fact, Saint Peter,

If you know what I mean, they haven't yet learned
How to be reverent.

Casehistory: Julie (encephalitis)

She stands between us. Her dress
Is zipped up back to front.
She has been crying her eyes
Dark. Her legs are thinner than legs.

She is importunate.

I'm not mental, am I?
Someone told me I was mental,
But I lost me memory
'Cos our dad died.
It don't make sense though, do it?
After I've been a nurse.

Her speech is nothing.

If I been rude, I apologize.
I lost me memory
'Cos I had the flu, didn't I?
I thought it was 'cos our dad died, see.
But it was 'cos I had the flu.

What imports this song?

Married? O god forgive me.
Who to? Let's be fair,
If you're getting married,
You ought to know the man.
O, not Roy!
I didn't marry him, did I?
I must be mental.
I'll do meself in.

There is a willow.

He was different to my brothers.
God forgive me for saying this,
He was like a woman.
Children? O god, please help me,
Please do, god.

O rose of May.

I'm getting better,
The doctor told me so,
As god's me witness, touch wood.
O, I am hungry.
I hope you don't mind me asking,
Where's the toilet to?

Do you see this, O God?

What about me dad?
Me dad's not gone, is he?

Casehistory: Alison (head injury)

(She looks at her photograph)

I would like to have known
My husband's wife, my mother's only daughter.
A bright girl she was.

Enmeshed in comforting
Fat, I wonder at her delicate angles.
Her autocratic knee

Like a Degas dancer's
Adjusts to the observer with airy poise,
That now lugs me upstairs

Hardly. Her face, broken
By nothing sharper than smiles, holds in its smiles
What I have forgotten.

She knows my father's dead,
And grieves for it, and smiles. She has digested
Mourning. Her smile shows it.

I, who need reminding
Every morning, shall never get over what
I do not remember.

Consistency matters.
I should like to keep faith with her lack of faith,
But forget her reasons.

Proud of this younger self,
I assert her achievements, her A levels,
Her job with a future.

Poor clever girl! I know,
For all my damaged brain, something she doesn't:
I am her future.

A bright girl she was.

Patience Strong

Everyone knows her name. Trite calendars
Of rose-nooked cottages or winding ways
Display her sentiments in homespun verse
Disguised as prose. She has her tiny niche
In women's magazines, too, tucked away
Among the recipes or near the end
Of some perennial serial. Her theme
Always the same: rain falls in every life,
But rainbows, bluebirds, spring, babies or God
Lift up our hearts. No doubt such rubbish sells.
She must be feathering her inglenook.
Genuine poets seldom coin the stuff,
Nor do they flaunt such aptly bogus names.
Their message is oblique; it doesn't fit
A pocket diary's page; nor does it pay.

One day in epileptic out-patients,
A working-man, a fellow in his fifties,
Was feeling bad. I brought a cup of tea.
He talked about his family and job:
His dad was in the Ambulance Brigade;
He hoped to join, but being epileptic,
They wouldn't have him. *Naturally*, he said,
With my disease, I'd be a handicap.
But I'd have liked to help. He sucked his tea,
Then from some special inner pocket brought
A booklet muffled up in cellophane,
Unwrapped it gently, opened at a page –
Characteristic cottage garden, seen
Through chintzy casement windows. Underneath
Some cosy musing in the usual vein,
And *See*, he said, *this is what keeps me going*.

After Visiting Hours

Like gulls they are still calling –
*I'll come again Tuesday. Our Dad
Sends his love.* They diminish, are gone.
Their world has received them,

As our world confirms us. Their debris
Is tidied into vases, lockers, minds.
We become pulses; mouthpieces
Of thermometers and bowels.

The trolley's rattle dispatches
The last lover. Now we can relax
Into illness, and reliably abstracted
Nurses will straighten our sheets,

Reorganize our symptoms. Outside,
Darkness descends like an eyelid.
It rains on our nearest and dearest
In car-parks, at bus-stops.

Now the bed-bound rehearse
Their repertoire of movements,
The dressing-gowned shuffle, clutching
Their glass bodies.

Now siren voices whisper
From headphones, and vagrant
Doctors appear, wreathed in stethoscopes
Like South Sea dancers.

All's well, all's quiet as the great
Ark noses her way into night,
Caulked, battened, blessed for her trip,
And behind, the gulls crying.

Ridge House (Old People's Home)

Something dramatic ought to happen here.
These pools and pergolas, these long dim fish
Anticipate an entrance, and offstage
Butler and parlourmaid are polishing
Silver and dialogue impartially.
Edwardian high comedy, of course.
Epigrams fidget in the atmosphere.

The trees are close, too. Something might draw near
Under the dead beech leaves. A cloven foot
Moves otherwise than ours, and makes less noise.
The shadowed lawn looks knowing. Grass, of course,
Has contacts with the supernatural.
At night, perhaps, when no one is about,
Oberon's cavalry manoeuvre here.

But all's quiet now. The August sky is clear,
Wisteria hangs its leaflets undisturbed.
The weather and the garden both deserve
A compliment, but no one's here, of course,
Except a sexless, ageless, shapeless shape,
Hunched underneath the cedar, muffled, rugged,
Which cannot see or smell, touch, taste or hear.

Dramatist to this house is Death. Austere,
Withdrawn, the scripts he writes. A single bed
Is his theatre. There the actor lies
Alone, and in the long dim hours explores
Dissolving senses. No one cares, of course.
The garden and the weather stay remote;
No god leaps from the clouds to interfere.

Stanton Drew

First you dismantle the landscape.
Take away everything you first
Thought of. Trees must go,
Roads, of course, the church,
Houses, hedges, livestock, a wire
Fence. The river can stay,
But loses its stubby fringe
Of willows. What do you
See now? Grass, the circling
Mendip rim, with its notches
Fresh, like carving. A sky
Like ours, but empty along
Its lower levels. And earth
Stripped of its future, tilted
Into meaning by these stones,
Pitted and unemphatic. Re-create them.
They are the most permanent
Presences here, but cattle, weather,
Archaeologists have rubbed against them.
Still in season they will
Hold the winter sun poised
Over Maes Knoll's white cheek,
Chain the moon's footsteps to
The pattern of their dance.
Stand inside the circle. Put
Your hand on stone. Listen
To the past's long pulse.

Earthed

Not precisely, like a pylon or
A pop-up toaster, but in a general
Way, stuck in the mud.

Not budding out of it like gipsies,
Laundry lashed to a signpost, dieting on
Nettles and hedgehogs,

Not lodged in its layers like badgers,
Tuned to the runes of its home-made walls, wearing
Its shape like a skin,

Not even securely rooted, like
Tribesmen tied to the same allotment, sure of
The local buses,

But earthed for all that, in the chalky
Kent mud, thin sharp ridges between wheel-tracks, in
Surrey's wild gravel,

In serious Cotswold uplands, where
Limestone confines the verges like yellow teeth,
And trees look sideways.

Everything from the clouds downwards holds
Me in its web, like the local newspapers,
Routinely special,

Or Somerset belfries, so highly
Parochial that Gloucestershire has none, or
Literate thrushes,

Conscientiously practising the
Phrases Browning liked, the attitude Hughes noticed,
Or supermarkets

Where the cashiers' rudeness is native
To the district, though the bread's not, or gardens,
Loved more than children,

Bright with resourcefulness and smelling
Of rain. This narrow island charged with echoes
And whispers snares me.

The Quiet Grave

(*for Cecil Sharp*)

Underground Rome waited solidly
In stone patience. Orpheus might lose
A beast or two, cracked apart by roots
Of brambled centuries, but still
Foundations lasted, knowing, like the princess,
That one day a ferret and a boy
Exploring a rabbithole would find an empire.

But this was a kingdom that lived

Some kinds of earth are reliable. The black
Peat of Somerset, and Norfolk mud
That tenderly cradled the deathship's spectral
Longrotted timbers. Some kinds of dryasdust
Air, too, responsibly cherish papyrus.

But this was a kingdom that lived
In the living air

Who held the keys of the kingdom?
Unfriendly old men in workhouses;
Bedridden ninety-year-olds terrorized
By highhanded grandchildren; gipsy women
With the long memories of the illiterate;
Old sailors who could sing only
Within sound of the sea. These
Held the keys of the kingdom.

Where was the kingdom?
The kingdom was everywhere. Under the noses
Of clerics devoted to folklore it lived
Invisibly, in gardens, in fields and kitchens,
In the servants' quarters. No one could find it
But those who were in it already.

When was the kingdom?
The kingdom was while women washed
And men broke stones. It was
Intervals in birdscaring; between
A cup too low and a cup
Too high; when a great-grandfather
Sang like a lark. Then
Was the kingdom.

Who cared for the kingdom?
An old woman gathering stones,
Who seized Sharp by his gentle-
Manly lapels, blowing her song into his mind
Through wrinkled gums. A surly chap
In Bridgwater Union, holding
Sharp's hand between his own grim bones,
Tears falling on all three. These
Cared for the kingdom.

What were the treasures of the kingdom?
Scraps of other worlds, prized
For their strangeness. A derrydown and a heyho,
And a rue dum day and a fol the diddle dee.
These were the treasures of the kingdom.

Who were the heirs of the kingdom?
The kingdom had no heirs, only
A younger generation that winked
At senility's music, and switched on the gramophone.

What was the end of the kingdom?
Massed choirs of the Federation
Of Women's Institutes filling
The Albert Hall; laconic
Improper poetry improved
For the benefit of schools;
Expansion of the Folk Song Industry. These
Were the end of the kingdom.

For this was a kingdom that lived
In the dying air

My Brother's House

Stood, like a fairytale, at the start
Of a wood. Vague fogs of bluebells
Absentmindedly invested it in summer.

Curdled dollops of snow
Flopped slowly in winter from invisible
Outstretched branches of firtrees.

The wood was a real wood, and
You could get lost in it. The trees
Had no names or numbers.

Jays, foxes and squirrels
Lived there. Also an obelisk in an odd
Corner, where nobody went.

The road to my brother's house
Had an air of leading nowhere. Visitors
Retreated, thinking of their back axles.

Blackberries and fifty-seven varieties
Of weeds had their eye on the garden.
Every year they shrivelled in flame,

Every day they returned unemphatic,
Not bothering to flaunt so
Easy a triumph. There was no garage

To uphold suburban standards, only
A shed where bicycles cowered among drips.
Indoors, all doors were always open

Or else jammed. Having a bath
Invited crowds, not just of spiders. Cats
Landed on chests with a thump and a yowl

In mid-dream. Overhead the patter of tiny
Paws or dense whirring of wings.
There were more humans around, too,

Than you quite expected, living furtive
Separate lives in damp rooms. Meals, haphazard
And elaborate, happened when, abandoning hope,

You had surrendered to bread
And butter. Massed choirs sang solidly
Through the masses of Haydn. Shoppers

Returned from forays with fifteen
Kinds of liversausage and no sugar.
When the family left, rats, rain and nettles

Took over instantly. I regret the passing
Of my brother's house. It was like living in Rome
Before the barbarians.

Only a Small Death

Only a small death, of course,
Not the full ceremony with mourners, a hearse,
Residuary legatees and a beanfeast
After the crematorium. Just a small, fully-
Conscious end.

Never again will you sleep in
This room, see sun rise through glass at this
Familiar angle, never again
Adjust to the shape of this bath, the smell
Of this cupboard.

You have died suddenly. The arrival
Of undertakers informs you of your
Decease. Their muscular detachment dissolves
Bonds between chairs and rooms, shelves
And their books.

The house offers its own valuation
Of the late owner. Dirt appears
In embarrassing contexts. If you were still
Alive, you would feel the need
To apologize.

Casual adjuncts of ordinary
Living, dustbins and drains, the
Unremarkable milkman, haloed in
The otherworldly glare of the last rites,
Achieve reality

Just as you end with them for ever.
Neighbours, paying a deathbed visit,
Acquire the tender resonance of friends,
But die as you go, birth exists on the edge
Of extinction.

The heir, arriving tactlessly early,
Retires till you finish dying. With you go
Archaic patterns of a home you will never
Come home to. Like an amputation, it will
Haunt you in the grave.

Not My Best Side

(*Uccello*: S. George and the Dragon, *The National Gallery*)

I
Not my best side, I'm afraid.
The artist didn't give me a chance to
Pose properly, and as you can see,
Poor chap, he had this obsession with
Triangles, so he left off two of my
Feet. I didn't comment at the time
(What, after all, are two feet
To a monster?) but afterwards
I was sorry for the bad publicity.
Why, I said to myself, should my conqueror
Be so ostentatiously beardless, and ride
A horse with a deformed neck and square hoofs?
Why should my victim be so
Unattractive as to be inedible,
And why should she have me literally
On a string? I don't mind dying
Ritually, since I always rise again,
But I should have liked a little more blood
To show they were taking me seriously.

II
It's hard for a girl to be sure if
She wants to be rescued. I mean, I quite
Took to the dragon. It's nice to be
Liked, if you know what I mean. He was
So nicely physical, with his claws
And lovely green skin, and that sexy tail,
And the way he looked at me,
He made me feel he was all ready to
Eat me. And any girl enjoys that.
So when this boy turned up, wearing machinery,
On a really *dangerous* horse, to be honest,
I didn't much fancy him. I mean,
What was he like underneath the hardware?
He might have acne, blackheads or even

28

Bad breath for all I could tell, but the dragon –
Well, you could see all his equipment
At a glance. Still, what could I do?
The dragon got himself beaten by the boy,
And a girl's got to think of her future.

III
I have diplomas in Dragon
Management and Virgin Reclamation.
My horse is the latest model, with
Automatic transmission and built-in
Obsolescence. My spear is custom-built,
And my prototype armour
Still on the secret list. You can't
Do better than me at the moment.
I'm qualified and equipped to the
Eyebrow. So why be difficult?
Don't you want to be killed and/or rescued
In the most contemporary way? Don't
You want to carry out the roles
That sociology and myth have designed for you?
Don't you realize that, by being choosy,
You are endangering job-prospects
In the spear- and horse-building industries?
What, in any case, does it matter what
You want? You're in my way.

Horticultural Show

These are Persephone's fruits
Of the underyear. These will guide us
Through the slow dream of winter.

Onions her paleskinned lamps.
Rub them for strange knowledge. They shine
With the light of the tomb.

Drawn in fine runes along
Hard green rinds, the incomprehensible
Initiation of the marrow.

All orange energy driven
Down to a final hair, these carrots
Have been at the heart of darkness.

And parti-coloured leeks,
Their green hair plaited, like Iroquois braves,
Leaning exhausted in corners.

Holystoned the presence
Of potatoes, pure white and stained pink.
Persephone's bread.

Sacrificed beetroots
Display their bleeding hearts. We read
The future in these entrails.

Out in the world excitable
Ponies caper, Punch batters Judy, a man
Creates a drystone wall in thirty minutes,

Arrows fly, coconuts fall, crocodiles
And Jubilee mugs, disguised as children,
Cope with candyfloss, the band
Adds its slow waltz heart beat.

Here in the tent, in the sepia hush,
Persephone's fruits utter where they have been,
Where we are going.

Men on Allotments

As mute as monks, tidy as bachelors,
They manicure their little plots of earth.
Pop music from the council house estate
Counterpoints with the Sunday-morning bells,
But neither siren voice has power for these
Drab solitary men who spend their time
Kneeling, or fetching water, soberly,
Or walking softly down a row of beans.

Like drill-sergeants, they measure their recruits.
The infant sprig receives the proper space
The manly fullgrown cauliflower will need.
And all must toe the line here; stem and leaf,
As well as root, obey the rule of string.
Domesticated tilth aligns itself
In sweet conformity; but head in air
Soars the unruly loveliness of beans.

They visit hidden places of the earth
When tenderly with fork and hand they grope
To lift potatoes, and the round, flushed globes
Tumble like pearls out of the moving soil.
They share strange intuitions, know how much
Patience and energy and sense of poise
It takes to be an onion; and they share
The subtle benediction of the beans.

They see the casual holiness that spreads
Along obedient furrows. Cabbages
Unfurl their veined and rounded fans in joy,
And buds of sprouts rejoice along their stalks.
The ferny tops of carrots, stout red stems
Of beetroot, zany sunflowers with blond hair
And bloodshot faces, shine like seraphim
Under the long flat fingers of the beans.

Canal: 1977

I remember this place: the conspiratorial
Presence of trees, the leaves' design
On uncommitted water, the pocky stonework
Ruining mildly in mottled silence,
The gutted pub, the dropping sounds
Inside the tunnel. I remember this place.

And before. I remember the sly lurchers,
The rose-and-castled barges, serious horses,
Coal smell, the leggers' hollow whoops
Down water, the bankrupt contractors
Grizzling into their beer, the trees and grass
Waiting to take over. I remember before.

And I remember the not-yet after,
When the money's raised and the sparetime Sunday
Navvying's over, the last intrusive sapling
Is ashes, when the bunting has bobbed, the first
Distinguished head ducked under the keystone,
There will be an after to be remembered

As the pleasurecraft purr their idle way
Into sunshine, and the smooth pink families
With their superior dogs enjoy the water,
The weather, the picturesque antiquity
That savaged so many who made it.
I remember after. And after

And before, the mute persistence of water
And grass and trees. Humanity goes out
Like a light, like the Roman-candle miners,
Shafting their pits on a donkey-winch, astraddle
A powderkeg, light in their teeth, a fuse in each pocket,
Lying foreign and broken in Gloucestershire churchyards now.

Palimpsest

Once the surface of the ground has been
The sidelong eyes of dawn and twilight
disturbed, the effect is, for all practical
catch in the net of their long shadows
purposes, permanent: the perfect
what is no longer there: grass offers
vestigia of a temple, as
its mute sermon on earth's derangement,
easily discernible in the
invisible and indelible
corn as on paper.
as children's hatred.

FROM *Standing To*

STATIONS UNDERGROUND

1. Fanfare

(*for Winifrid Fanthorpe, born 5 February 1895, died 13 November 1978*)

You, in the old photographs, are always
The one with the melancholy half-smile, the one
Who couldn't quite relax into the joke.

My extrovert dog of a father,
With his ragtime blazer and his swimming togs
Tucked like a swiss roll under his arm,
Strides in his youth towards us down some esplanade,

Happy as Larry. You, on his other arm,
Are anxious about the weather forecast,
His overdraft, or early closing day.

You were good at predicting failure: marriages
Turned out wrong because you said they would.
You knew the rotations of armistice and war,
Watched politicians' fates with gloomy approval.

All your life you lived in a minefield,
And were pleased, in a quiet way, when mines
Exploded. You never actually said
I told you so, but we could tell you meant it.

Crisis was your element. You kept your funny stories,
Your music-hall songs for doodlebug and blitz-nights.
In the next cubicle, after a car-crash, I heard you
Amusing the nurses with your trench wit through the blood.

Magic alerted you. Green, knives and ladders
Will always scare me through your tabus.
Your nightmare was Christmas; so much organized
Compulsory whoopee to be got through.

You always had some stratagem for making
Happiness keep its distance. Disaster
Was what you planned for. You always
Had hoarded loaves or candles up your sleeve.

Houses crumbled around your ears, taps leaked,
Electric light bulbs went out all over England,
Because for you homes were only provisional,
Bivouacs on the stony mountain of living.

You were best at friendship with chars, gipsies,
Or very far-off foreigners. Well-meaning neighbours
Were dangerous because they lived near.

Me too you managed best at a distance. On the landline
From your dugout to mine, your nightly
Pass, friend was really often quite jovial.

You were the lonely figure in the doorway
Waving goodbye in the cold, going back to a sink-full
Of crockery dirtied by those you loved. We
Left you behind to deal with our crusts and gristle.

I know why you chose now to die. You foresaw
Us approaching the Delectable Mountains,
And didn't feel up to all the cheers and mafficking.

But how, dearest, will even you retain your
Special brand of hard-bitten stoicism
Among the halleluyas of the triumphant dead?

2. *Four Dogs*

1. CERBERUS

The first was known simply
As *the dog*. Later writers gave him a name,
Three heads, a collar of serpents,
And a weakness for cake.
They also claimed he could be
Calmed by magic, charmed by music,
And even, on one occasion, thrashed.

Later writers can seldom be trusted.
Primary sources are more reliable:
This dog guarded his master's gate,
Wagged his ears and tail at visitors,
Admitted them all, and saw to it
That nobody ever got out.

2. ANUBIS

The civil Egyptians made
Their dog half man. The dog end
Had the usual doggy tastes
For digging, and bones. But the human half
Was drawn to conservation and chemistry,
Liked pickling, preserving, dissecting,
Distillation; added artistry
To the dog's enthusiasm. Undertaking
Became Egyptian art.

3. EL PERRO (GOYA)

There was a man who never blinked.
Helmeted in deafness, he set down
What he saw: the unembarrassed beastliness
Of humanity, country picnics, rape,
Blank-faced politicians, idiot obstinate kings,
Famine, firing-squads, milkmaids.
He charted nightmare's dominion
On his house's walls. To him appeared
The thing itself, snouting its way
Up from underground. He drew it
As it was: darkness, a dog's head,
Mild, mongrel, appalling.

4. SHANDY

The fourth dog lives in my house with me
Like a sister, loves me doggedly,
Guiltily, abstractedly; disobeys me
When I am not looking. I love her
Abstractedly, guiltily; feed her; try
Not to let her know she reminds me
Of the other dogs.

3. At the Ferry

Laconic as anglers and, like them, submissive,
The grey-faced loiterers on the bank,
Charon, of your river.

They are waiting their turn. Nothing we do
Distracts them much. It was you, Charon, I saw,
Refracted in a woman's eyes.

Patient, she sat in a wheelchair,
In an X-ray department, waiting for someone
To do something to her,

Given a magazine, folded back
At the problem page: *What should I do*
About my husband's impotence?

Is a registry office marriage
Second-best? I suffer from a worrying
Discharge from my vagina.

In her hands she held the thing obediently;
Obediently moved her eyes in the direction
Of the problems of the restless living.

But her mind deferred to another dimension.
Outward bound, tenderly inattentive, she was waiting,
Charon, for you.

And the nineteen-stone strong man, felled
By his spawning brain, lying still to the sound
Of the DJ's brisk chirrup;

He wasn't listening, either. He was on the lookout
For the flurry of water as your craft
Comes about in the current.

I saw you once, boatman, lean by your punt-pole
On an Oxford river, in the dubious light
Between willow and water,

Where I had been young and lonely, being
Now loved, and older; saw you in the tender, reflective
Gaze of the living

Looking down at me, deliberate,
And strange in the half-light, saying nothing,
Claiming me, Charon, for life.

4. Rising Damp

(for C. A. K. and R. K. M.)

'A river can sometimes be diverted, but it is a very hard thing to lose
it altogether.'
       J. G. Head, paper read to the Auctioneers' Institute in 1907

At our feet they lie low,
The little fervent underground
Rivers of London

Effra, Graveney, Falcon, Quaggy,
Wandle, Walbrook, Tyburn, Fleet

Whose names are disfigured,
Frayed, effaced.

These are the Magogs that chewed the clay
To the basin that London nestles in.
These are the currents that chiselled the city,
That washed the clothes and turned the mills,
Where children drank and salmon swam
And wells were holy.

They have gone under.
Boxed, like the magician's assistant.
Buried alive in earth.
Forgotten, like the dead.

They return spectrally after heavy rain,
Confounding suburban gardens. They infiltrate
Chronic bronchitis statistics. A silken
Slur haunts dwellings by shrouded
Watercourses, and is taken
For the footing of the dead.

Being of our world, they will return
(Westbourne, caged at Sloane Square,
Will jack from his box),
Will deluge cellars, detonate manholes,
Plant effluent on our faces,
Sink the city.

Effra, Graveney, Falcon, Quaggy,
Wandle, Walbrook, Tyburn, Fleet

It is the other rivers that lie
Lower, that touch us only in dreams
That never surface. We feel their tug
As a dowser's rod bends to the source below

Phlegethon, Acheron, Lethe, Styx.

5. Sisyphus

'The struggle itself towards the heights is enough to fill a man's
heart. One must imagine Sisyphus happy.'

Camus, *The Myth of Sisyphus*

Apparently I rank as one
Of the more noteworthy sights down here.
As to that, I can't judge, having
No time to spare for tourists.

My preoccupations are this stone
And this hill. I have to push
The one up the other.

A trivial task for a team, an engine,
A pair of horses. The interest lies
Not in the difficulty of the doing,

But the difficulty for the doer. I accept this
As my vocation: to do what I cannot do.
The stone and I are

Close. I know its every wart, its ribby ridges,
Its snags, its lips. And the stone knows me,
Cheek, chin and shoulders, elbow, groin, shin, toe,
Muscle, bone, cartilage and muddied skinprint,
My surfaces, my angles and my levers.

The hill I know by heart too,
Have studied incline, foothold, grain,
With watchmaker's patience.

Concentration is mutual. The hill
Is hostile to the stone and me.
The stone resents me and the hill.

But I am the mover. I cannot afford
To spend energy on emotion. I push
The stone up the hill. At the top

It falls, and I pursue it,
To heave it up again. Time not spent
On doing this is squandered time.

The gods must have had a reason
For setting me this task. I have forgotten it,
And I do not care.

6. The Guide

The level-headed Greeks grasped
Their underworld, and charted it. Rivers,
Hills and dry land behaved
Geographically, appropriately. Sentence
Was passed by a panel
Of High Court Judges, with an assessor
To help with hard cases,
And the terrain, being logical,
Enforced the law.

Dante the bureaucrat invented
A new filing system for
The irregular dead, pigeon-holing them
As pertinently as the Mikado.
They fluttered and squeaked,
But he netted and mounted them,
Steady as Aristotle, knowing
The unutterable articulations of peace,
From purgatory to paradise, were based
On the accurate taxonomy of sin.

Dispossession, and the secrets
Of his beemaster father,
Taught Vergil more than men know.
He trudged further into suffering
And pity than other people,
Led to accept his vocation
By the annals of the hive. He knew
How drones die nobly
In midsummer air after mating,
Or sombrely, autumnal offerings;
How the workforce fly their wings
To rags, to death; how virgin knights
Are stabbed in their royal cradles;
How tired and failing monarchs
Undertake forced marches upcountry

To found new colonies. He knew
That the bees' god is the Future,
Which consumes first the loving,
The wise, the beautiful, the brave,
Because they are special, and favours
The ordinary bee, the bee-in-the-air,
Aeneas, the survivor.
So Orpheus has to die. So Rome
Goes on, as Vergil knew it would,
Monumentally second-rate city.

About Hell, too, he knew more
Than the others. Through blunt-edged Latin,
Its meanings scuffed by ages of misuse,
He found ways of wording the unsayable,
Fathomed echo-chambers behind the dulled
And vague, and told us:
Hell is a sort of underground bog.
There are no landmarks. In it
Those we have loved and failed
Turn their backs for ever.

7. *The Passing of Alfred*

'He [Tennyson] died with his hand on his Shakespeare, and the
moon shining full into the window over him . . . A worthy end.'

Queen Victoria, *Journal*

Our fathers were good at dying.
They did it lingeringly,
As if they liked it; correctly,
With earnest attention to detail,
Codicils brought up to date,
Forgiveness, confession, last-gasp
Penitence properly witnessed
By responsible persons. Attorneys,
Clerics, physicians, all knew their place
In the civil pavane of dying.

Households discharged
Their methodical duties: said farewell
In order of precedence, outdoor staff first,
Faithful hounds respectfully mourning,
Lastly the widow-to-be, already
Pondering a transformed wardrobe.

They died in the houses,
The beds they were born in,
They died where they lived, between
Known sheets, to the obbligato
Of familiar creaks and ticks.

We who differ, whose dears are absorbed
Into breezy wards for routine terminations,
Envy our fathers their decorous endings
In error. Nothing makes extinction easy.
They also died appallingly, over
The family breakfast-cups; bloodily
In childbed; graveyard coughed themselves
Into coffins; declined from heart-break
And hunger. And however resigned,
Orderly, chaste, aesthetic the passing of Alfred,
Remorse, regret still shadowed the living after.

Like us they ran from habit to tell good news
To dead ears; like us they dreamed
Of childhood, and being forgiven;
And the dead followed them, as they do us,
Tenderly through darkness,
But fade when we turn to look in the upper air.

ONLY HERE FOR THE BIER

I wrote these four poems because I was interested to see how the masculine world of Shakespeare's tragedies would look from the woman's angle. In fact, women exist in this world only to be killed, as sacrificial victims. So I imagined Gertrude (mother-in-law), Regan (king's daughter), Emilia (army wife) and the un-named waiting gentlewoman in *Macbeth* having a chat with some usual female confidante, like a hairdresser, or a telephone.

– U. A. F.

1. Mother-in-law

Such a nice girl. Just what I wanted
For the boy. Not top drawer, you know,
But so often, in our position, that
Turns out to be a mistake. They get
The ideas of their station, and that upsets
So many applecarts. The lieges, of course,
Are particularly hidebound, and the boy,
For all his absentminded ways, is a great one
For convention. Court mourning, you know . . .
Things like that. We don't want a Brunhilde
Here. But she was so suitable. Devoted
To her father and brother, and,
Of course, to the boy. And a very
Respectable, loyal family. Well, loyal
To number two, at any rate. Number one,
I remember, never quite trusted . . . Yes,
And had just the right interests. Folk song, for instance,
(Such a sweet little voice), and amateur
Dramatics. Inherited *that* taste
From her father. Dear old fellow, he'd go on
For hours about his college drama group.
And the boy's so keen on the stage. It's nice
When husband and wife have a shared interest,
Don't you think? Then botany. Poor little soul,
She was really keen. We'd go for trips
With the vasculum, and have such fun
Asking the lieges their country names for flowers.
Some of them, my dear, were scarcely delicate
(The names, I mean), but the young nowadays
Don't seem to notice. Marriage
Would have made her more innocent, of course.
I can't think who will do for the boy now.
I seem to be the only woman left round here.

2. King's Daughter

Being the middle sister is tiresome.
The rawboned heroics of the eldest
Are out of reach; so is the youngest's
Gamine appeal. It is impossible for the second child
To be special. One must just cultivate
One's own garden, neatly. For neatness and order
Matter in the world of the middle daughter,
The even number. Disorderly lives
Are distasteful. Adultery is untidy;
Servants should be accurate and invisible.
Individuals should have two eyes, or none;
One eye is unacceptable. I enjoy the beauty
Of formality, and have no objection
To offering father the elaborate rhetoric
He expects. There is a certain correctness
In the situation. One must object, however,
To the impropriety of those who propose
Different rules. One is no innovator:
Innovation is unfeminine. It is important
That ashtrays should be emptied, and always
In the same place, that meals be punctual.
One depends on one's servants to supply
Visual and temporal symmetry. Equally,
One relies on one's family to support
The proper structure of relationships. It is a pity
That one's father is so eccentric, that his friends
Are the sort of people one tries not to know,
That one's sisters are, in their different ways,
Both so unwomanly. One would never dream
Of asserting oneself in public, as they do.
One tries to cultivate the woman's touch.

3. Army Wife

It's the place, I think. Everyone seems
To have gone to pieces here. Oh, not me,
My dear. I'm so used to the life. Just
Dump me down anywhere, and I'd make
A go of it – with reasonable living quarters,
Mind you, and good native servants.
Can't do without them! No, I don't count myself,
Nor Jim, of course. Jim keeps his cool
Whatever happens. We're old campaigners.
But take Mike. Such an awfully nice chap.
The new sort of officer, has a degree,
Staff College, all that sort of thing,
But absolutely no side. We think the world
Of Mike. So what does the silly ass do
But get himself mixed up with a native tart
(Very flashy girl – you've probably seen her around),
And a drunk-and-disorderly, and – oh, it's too shaming.
What the locals must be thinking! Mind you,
I blame the CO for all this. I know he's brilliant
In the field, but he *isn't* one of us, whatever
They may say. What's bred in the bone . . .
And somehow, here he's more noticeable.
There was that dreadful scene he made yesterday
About the laundry, and goodness knows
He ought to leave things like that
To his batman. Keeps a sword in his wardrobe,
They tell me. Yes, extraordinary, isn't it? A bit –
Well – *native*. And dear little Mrs CO –
Yes, isn't she a darling? Terribly good family,
But absolutely no side – she really has no idea
How to cope. I said to Jim, the trouble with you boys
Is, you need an enemy. Now the Wogs
Have packed up and gone home, you've simply
Nothing to do, so you get into trouble.
But Jim'll be all right. Jim keeps his cool
Whatever happens.

4. Waiting Gentlewoman

If Daddy had known the setup,
I'm absolutely positive, he'd never
Have let me come. Honestly,
The whole thing's too gruesome
For words. There's nobody here to talk to
At all. Well, nobody under about ninety,
I mean. All the possible men have buggered
Off to the other side, and the rest,
Poor old dears, they'd have buggered off
Too, if their poor old legs would have
Carried them. HM's a super person, of course,
But she's a bit seedy just now,
Quite different from how marvellous she was
At the Coronation. And this doctor they've got in –
Well, he's only an ordinary little GP,
With a very odd accent, and even I
Can see that what HM needs is
A real psychiatrist. I mean, all this
About *blood*, and *washing*. Definitely Freudian.
As for Himself, well, definitely
Not my type. Daddy's got this thing
About selfmade men, of course, that's why
He was keen for me to come. But I think
He's gruesome. What HM sees in him
I cannot imagine. *And* he talks to himself.
That's so rude, I always think.
I hope Daddy comes for me soon.

Inside

Inside our coloured, brisk world,
Like a bone inside a leg, lies
The world of the negative.

It is the same world, only somehow
Conviction has dribbled out of it,
Like stuffing from a toy.

A world of hypnotic clocks and unfinished
Goblin gestures. Nothing moves in a landscape
Fixed in hysteria's stasis.

This is the hushed network of nightmare.
You have lost touch with the sustaining
Ordinariness of things.

Suddenly the immense and venerable
Fallacies that prop the universe
Fail, the colossal flickering fabric
Which we must believe in so that it can be
Goes out.

Here malevolence is routine, the shadow
Is real and the world is shadow.
Here the happy-ever-after crumples
Into a rheumatoid *hic-iacet*.

Here the appalling and unexpected
Disaster is expected. Here the blood
Screams whispers to the flesh.

And here the alien wanders
Endless benighted streets where innocent households
Laugh behind blinds and believe in tomorrow
Like the milkbottles at the door.

The Conductor

I am the conductor. I preside
Over the players, clothed in the swagger
Of my office. My imperative hands
Ordain volume and tempo. I am
The music's master.

This is the music, propped open before me:
Immense Unfinished Symphony of life,
Its intervals, blunt naturals and fugues,
Its resolutions, syncopations, shakes,
Scored for my players.

These are the players. (Stand up, friends,
And make your bows.) A random lot,
Amateurs all, for nothing at all disbars,
And finally all find parts that fit them
For my orchestra.

Listen! an excerpt: today's programme.
First subject, in flute's paediatric whine,
Transposed now to the key of senility,
Dribbling urine and spittle, difficult heartbeats
Plucking like harpstrings.

Each virtuoso has his own variation:
Depression's largo, schizophrenia's scherzo,
Mute music of the withdrawn, epileptic cadenzas,
The plagal cadence of the stretcher-borne dying,
Drum taps of the blind.

Listen again. The second subject
Is harder to hear, is sensed at last
In pauses, breves, a *did-not-come*, a rest,
A silence. For this symphony's name
Is also Farewell,

And as each player reaches his part's end
He tucks his instrument decently under his arm,
Snuffs out his candle, tiptoes demurely away
Into the dark and the stillness. For him
The concert's over.

I, the receptionist, must also play
My part, and go. I shoot my cuffs,
And watch my hectoring fingers, like the rest,
Sprout into rattlebones. And see
A new conductor,

Young, fetching, shifty, immortal,
Hermes bringer of dreams, the light-fingered,
Hermes who leads men's souls in another direction
From our world of unholy living
And wholly dying.

Lament for the Patients

These were far from lovely in their lives,
And when they died, they were instantly forgotten.

These were the permanent patients, the ones
Whose disease was living. Their trophy, death,
Being to no one's advantage, was kept dark.

These had quiet funerals (*no flowers,
Please*), silent incinerations, hushed-up autopsies;
Their dying figured in obituary columns
Of local papers only.

On these specialists had practised specialities;
Had weighed and measured; had taken samples
Of blood and urine; had tested IQs,
Reflexes, patience; had applied
Shock treatment, drugs and nice hot cups of tea.

Of these specialists had washed their hands,
Having failed to arrive at a satisfactory
Diagnosis (anglicè: having failed to infect them
With a reason for living). Therefore they died.

To me came the news of their dying:
From the police (*Was this individual
A patient of yours?*); from ambulance
Control (*Our team report this patient
You sent us to fetch is deceased already*);
From tight-lipped telephoning widowers
(*My wife died in her sleep last night*);
From carboned discharge letters (*I note
That you have preserved the brain. We would certainly
Be very interested in this specimen*);
From curt press cuttings (*Man found dead.
Foul play not suspected*). I annotated their notes
With their final symptom: *died.*
Therefore I remember them.

These I remember:
Sonia, David, Penny, who chose death.
Lynn and Gillian, who died undiagnosed.
Peter, whose death was enigmatic.
Simple Betty, who suddenly stopped living.
Lionhearted Gertrude, who persevered to the end.
Patricia, so sorry for herself,
For whom I was not sufficiently sorry.
Julian, the interesting case. Alan,
Broken by a lorry, resurrected by surgeons,
Who nevertheless contrived at length to die.

Not for these the proper ceremonies, the solemn crowds,
The stripped gun-carriage, the slow march from *Saul*,
The tumulus, the friendly possessions
At hand in the dark. Not even
The pauper's deal coffin, brief office
Of the uncared-for. Only the recital
Of disembodied voices in a clerk's ear,
A final emendation of the text.

Reports

Has made a sound beginning
Strikes the right note:
Encouraging, but dull.
Don't give them anything
To take hold of. Even
Pronouns are dangerous.

The good have no history,
So don't bother. *Satisfactory*
Should satisfy them.

Fair and *Quite good*,
Multi-purpose terms,
By meaning nothing,
Apply to all.
Feel free to deploy them.

Be on your guard;
Unmanageable oaf cuts both ways.
Finds the subject difficult,
Acquitting you, converts
Oaf into idiot, usher to master.

Parent, child, head,
Unholy trinity, will read
Your scripture backwards.
Set them no riddles, just
Echo the common-room cliché:
Must make more effort.

Remember your high calling:
School is the world.
Born at *Sound beginning*,
We move from *Satisfactory*
To *Fair*, then *Find*
The subject difficult,
Learning at last we
Could have done better.

Stone only, final instructor,
Modulates from the indicative
With *Rest in peace*.

Half-term

Always autumn, in my memory.
Butter ringing the drilled teashop crumpets;
Handmade chocolates, rich enough to choke you,
Brought in special smooth paper from Town.

(Back at school, the square tall piles
Of bread, featureless red jam in basins,
Grace, a shuffle of chairs, the separate table
For the visiting lacrosse team.)

Long awkward afternoons in hotel lounges,
Islanded in swollen armchairs, eyeing
Aristocratic horses in irrelevant magazines.
Should I be talking to Them?

(Back at school the raptly selfish
Snatch at self: the clashing
Determined duets in cold practising-
Rooms, the passionate solitary knitting.)

Inadequacies of presentation, perceived
By parents' temporary friends; hair, manners,
Clothes, have failed to adjust.
I don't know the rules of snooker.

(Back at school, the stiff reliable
Awkwardnesses of work. History test
On Monday morning. Deponent verbs.
I have never been good at maths.)

Saying goodbye. There are tears
And hugs, relief, regret. They,
Like me, return to a patterned life
Whose rules are easy. Unworthily

I shall miss chocolate, crumpets,
Comfort, but not the love I only
Sense as they go, waving to the end,
Vague in the streetlamps of November.

(Back at school the bullies,
Tyrants and lunatics are waiting.
I can deal with them.)

You will be hearing from us shortly

You feel adequate to the demands of this position?
What qualities do you feel you
Personally have to offer?

                                               Ah

Let us consider your application form.
Your qualifications, though impressive, are
Not, we must admit, precisely what
We had in mind. Would you care
To defend their relevance?

                                          Indeed

Now your age. Perhaps you feel able
To make your own comment about that,
Too? We are conscious ourselves
Of the need for a candidate with precisely
The right degree of immaturity.

                                  So glad we agree

And now a delicate matter: your looks.
You do appreciate this work involves
Contact with the actual public? Might they,
Perhaps, find your appearance
Disturbing?

                                     Quite so

And your accent. That is the way
You have always spoken, is it? What
Of your education? Were
You educated? We mean, of course,
Where were you educated?
                        And how
Much of a handicap is that to you,
Would you say?

                    Married, children,
We see. The usual dubious
Desire to perpetuate what had better
Not have happened at all. We do not
Ask what domestic disasters shimmer
Behind that vaguely unsuitable address.

And you were born – ?

                                        Yes. Pity.

So glad we agree.

BC:AD

This was the moment when Before
Turned into After, and the future's
Uninvented timekeepers presented arms.

This was the moment when nothing
Happened. Only dull peace
Sprawled boringly over the earth.

This was the moment when even energetic Romans
Could find nothing better to do
Than counting heads in remote provinces.

And this was the moment
When a few farm workers and three
Members of an obscure Persian sect

Walked haphazard by starlight straight
Into the kingdom of heaven.

The Contributors

Not your fault, gentlemen.
We acquit you of the calculatedly
Equivalent gift, the tinsel token.
Mary, maybe, fancied something more practical:
A layette, or at least a premium bond.
Firmly you gave the extravagantly
Useless, your present the unwrapped
Hard-edged stigma of vocation.

Not your fault, beasts,
Who donated your helpless animal
Rectitude to the occasion.
Not yours the message of the goblin
Robin, the red-nosed reindeer,
Nor had you in mind the yearly
Massacre of the poultry innocent,
Whom we judge correct for the feast.

Not your fault, Virgin,
Muddling along in the manger,
With your confused old man,
Your bastard baby, in conditions
No social worker could possibly approve.
How could your improvised, improvident
Holiness predict our unholy family Xmas,
Our lonely overdoses, deepfrozen bonhomie?

On Buying OS Sheet 163

I own all this. Not loutish acres
That tax the spirit, but the hawking
Eye's freehold, paper country.

Thirtytwo inches of aqueduct,
Windmill (disused), club house, embankment,
Public conveniences

In rural areas. This is my
Landlocked landscape that lives in cipher,
And is truer than walking.

Red and imperial, the Romans
Stride eastward. Mysterious, yellow,
The Salt Way halts and is gone.

Here, bigger than the hamlets they are,
Wild wayside syllables stand blooming:
Filkins, Lechlade, Broughton Poggs.

Here only I discard the umber
Reticulations of sad cities,
The pull and drag of mud.

Princetown

In the town it seems just a local
Joke, like piskies or Uncle Tom Cobley,
Though in rather poor taste. Souvenir mugs
Insistent as fat-bottomed mums on seaside postcards,
And tiny priapic men: *Property*
Of HM Prison, Dartmoor.
Not to be taken away. But if you walk
The ripped-up railway, its stonework
The patient, perfect carving of cheap labour,
To the quarries, you begin to imagine
The bald, tanned pates, grotesque livery,
Automatic warders, routine hopelessness,
But far off, historic, like walking
The Roman Wall, reconstructing
A massive alert garrison from piles
Of rubbish. So here, until, nearing the town,
We saw the discreet bulk, shining in twilight,
Each window equally watted. And I remembered
The mother and daughter, arm in arm and crying,
Outside the café offering cream teas.

Hang-gliders in January

(*for C. K.*)

Like all miracles, it has a rational
Explanation; and like all miracles, insists
On being miraculous. We toiled
In the old car up from the lacklustre valley,
Taking the dogs because somebody had to,
At the heel of a winter Sunday afternoon

Into a sky of shapes flying:
Pot-bellied, shipless sails, dragonflies towering
Still with motion, daytime enormous bats,
Titanic tropical fish, and men,
When we looked, men strapped to wings,
Men wearing wings, men flying

Over a landscape too emphatic
To be understood: humdrum fields
With hedges and grass, the mythical river,
Beyond it the forest, the foreign high country.
The exact sun, navigating downwards
To end the revels, and you, and me,
The dogs, even, enjoying a scamper,
Avoiding scuffles.

It was all quite simple, really. We saw
The aground flyers, their casques and belts
And defenceless legs; we saw the earthed wings
Being folded like towels; we saw
The sheepskin-coated wives and mothers
Loyally watching; we saw a known,
Explored landscape by sunset-light,

We saw for ourselves how it was done,
From takeoff to landing. But nothing cancelled
The cipher of the soaring, crucified men,
Which we couldn't unravel; which gave us
Also, somehow, the freedom of air. Not
In vast caravels, triumphs of engineering,
But as men always wanted, simply,
Like a bird at home in the sky.

Getting It Across

(*for Caroline*)

'His disciples said unto him, Lo, now speakest thou plainly, and
speakest no proverb. Now are we sure that thou knowest all things.'
St John 16:29–30

This is the hard thing.
Not being God, the Son of Man,
– I was born for that part –
But patiently incising on these yokel faces,
Mystified, bored and mortal,
The vital mnemonics they never remember.

There is enough of Man in my God
For me to construe their frowns. I feel
The jaw-cracking yawns they try to hide
When out I come with one of my old
Chestnuts. *Christ! not that bloody
Sower again*, they are saying, or *God!
Not the Prodigal fucking Son.
Give us a new one, for Messiah's sake.*

They know my unknowable parables as well
As each other's shaggy dog stories.
*I say! I say! I say! There was this Samaritan,
This Philistine and this Roman . . .* or
*What did the high priest say
To the belly dancer?* All they need
Is the cue for laughs. My sheep and goats,
Virgins, pigs, figtrees, loaves and lepers
Confuse them. Fishing, whether for fish or men,
Has unfitted them for analogy.

Yet these are my mouths. Through them only
Can I speak with Augustine, Aquinas, Martin, Paul,
Regius Professors of Divinity,
And you, and you.
How can I cram the sense of Heaven's kingdom
Into our pidgin-Aramaic quayside jargon?

I envy Moses, who could choose
The diuturnity of stone for waymarks
Between man and Me. He broke the tablets,
Of course. I too know the easy messages
Are the ones not worth transmitting;
But he could at least carve.
The prophets too, however luckless
Their lives and instructions, inscribed on wood,
Papyrus, walls, their jaundiced oracles.

I alone must write on flesh. Not even
The congenial face of my Baptist cousin,
My crooked affinity Judas, who understands,
Men who would give me accurately to the unborn
As if I were something simple, like bread.
But Pete, with his headband stuffed with fishhooks,
His gift for rushing in where angels wouldn't,
Tom, for whom metaphor is anathema,
And James and John, who want the room at the top –
These numskulls are my medium. I called them.

I am tattooing God on their makeshift lives.
My Keystone Cops of disciples, always
Running absurdly away, or lying ineptly,
Cutting off ears and falling into the water,
These Sancho Panzas must tread my Quixote life,
Dying ridiculous and undignified,
Flayed and stoned and crucified upside down.
They are the dear, the human, the dense, for whom
My message is. That might, had I not touched them,
Have died decent respectable upright deaths in bed.

Pomona and Vertumnus

Lady of kitchen-gardens, learned
In the ways of the early thin-skinned rhubarb,
Whose fingers fondle each gooseberry bristle,
Stout currants sagging on their flimsy stalks,
And sprinting strawberries, that colonize
As quick as Rome.

Goddess of verges, whose methodical
Tenderness fosters the vagrant croppers,
Gawky raspberry refugees from gardens,
Hip, sloe, juniper, blackberry, crab,
Humble abundance of heath, hedge, copse,
The layabouts' harvest.

Patron of orchards, pedantic observer
Of rites, of prune, graft, spray and pick,
In whose honour the Bramley's branches
Bow with their burly cargo, from grass-deep
To beyond ladders; you who teach pears their proper shape,
And brush the ripe plum's tip with a touch of crystal.

I know your lovers, earth's grubby godlings:
Silvanus, whose province is muck-heaps
And electric fences; yaffle-headed Picus;
Faunus the goatman. All of them friends
Of the mud-caked cattle, courting you gruffly
With awkward, touching gifts.

But I am the irrepressible, irresponsible
Spirit of Now: no constant past,
No predictable future. All my genius
Goes into moments. I have nothing to give
But contradiction and alteration.

74

Me, therefore, the wise goddess picked
When I came to her, true to my bent,
In the form of an old woman.

Janus

I am the two-headed anniversary god,
Lord of the Lupercal and the Letts diary.
I have a head for figures.

My clocks are the moon and sun,
My almanac the zodiac. The ticktock seasons,
The hushabye seas are under my thumb.

From All Saints to All Souls I celebrate
The *da capo* year. My emblems are albums,
The bride's mother's orchid corsage, the dark cortège.

Master of the silent passacaglia
Of the future, I observe the dancers,
But never teach them the step.

I am the birthday prescience
Who knows the obituary, the tombstone's arithmetic.
Not telling is my present.

I monitor love through its mutations
From paper to ruby. I am archivist
Of the last divorce and the first kiss.

I am director of the forgotten fiesta.
I know why men at Bacup black their faces;
Who horned at Abbots Bromley tread the mazes.

I am the future's overseer, the past's master.
See all, know all, speak not.
I am the two-faced god.

Genesis

(*for J. R. R. Tolkien*)

In the beginning were the words,
Aristocratic, cryptic, chromatic.
Vowels as direct as mid-day,
Consonants lanky as long-swords.

Mouths materialized to speak the words:
Leafshaped lips for the high language,
Tranquil tongues for the tree-creatures,
Slits and slobbers for the lower orders.

Deeds came next, words' children.
Legs by walking evolved a landscape.
Continents and chronologies occurred,
Complex and casual as an implication.

Arched over all, alarming nimbus,
Magic's disorderly thunder and lightning.

The sage sat in his suburban fastness,
Garrisoned against progress. He grieved
At what the Duke's men did to our words
(Whose war memorial is every signpost).

The sage sat. And middle-earth
Rose around him like a rumour.
Grave grammarians, Grimm and Werner,
Gave it laws, granted it charters.

The sage sat. But the ghosts walked
Of the Birmingham schoolboy, the Somme soldier,
Whose bones lay under the hobbit burrows,
Who endured darkness, and friends dying,

Whom words waylaid in a Snow Hill siding,
Coal truck pit names, grimy, gracious,
Blaen-Rhondda, *Nantyglo*, *Senghenydd*.
In these deeps middle-earth was mined.

These were the words in the beginning.

Father in the Railway Buffet

What are you doing here, ghost, among these urns,
These film-wrapped sandwiches and help-yourself biscuits,
Upright and grand, with your stick, hat and gloves,
Your breath of eau-de-cologne?

What have you to say to these head-scarfed tea-ladies,
For whom your expensive vowels are exotic as Japan?
Stay, ghost, in your proper haunts, the clubland smokerooms,
Where you know the waiters by name.

You have no place among these damp and nameless.
Why do you walk here? *I came to say goodbye.*
You were ashamed of me for being different.
It didn't matter.

You who never even learned to queue?

Portraits of Tudor Statesmen

Surviving is keeping your eyes open,
Controlling the twitchy apparatus
Of iris, white, cornea, lash and lid.

So the literal painter set it down –
The sharp raptorial look; strained eyeball;
And mail, ruff, bands, beard, anything, to hide
The violently vulnerable neck.

The Constant Tin Soldier

I. BREAKING DAY

Dying is easier.
Just a flick of somebody's finger,
Then the icy exactness of rigor mortis,
While posthumous flies and decorations settle,
A subaltern writes thirty-two letters
By torchlight to next of kin,
And the Germans advance in your boots,
Which are better than theirs.

It isn't always lucky to stay alive.
Some never recover from surviving.
The showy heraldry of scars excuses,
But not the chronic tic of terror,
Picked up on a foggy March morning
Between the Staffords and the Suffolks,
Between Bullecourt and Croisilles.
You will carry this day like a tumour
In your head for life, fusilier,
And no one will ever needle it out.

You remember the date:

21st March, 1918. Day
Of the Kaiserschlacht, day
Of the German Spring Offensive.
We, the beaten, have no name for that day
In our own language.

You remember your place:

Third Army, 34th Division,
102nd brigade. HQ Gomiecourt
(Which I never say) under
Lt Col Charlton (whom I never

81

Saw again after. Only now, sixty years on,
A youngster tells me he was taken prisoner.
I thought him killed).
23rd Northumberland Fusiliers.

You remember the weather:

Sun on the 20th, following rain
And squally winds. Enemy weathermen
Prophesied continuing calm. It would be safe,
They said, to use gas against us. Then
An intense, still morning; no wind;
But ground mist ghosting
To dense, inimical fog.

You remember the timing:

0440 hours: artillery bombardment begins.
Five hours of General Surprise Fire.
The German brass, guns, mortars and howitzers,
Jarring in unison. It rained noise,
Mud, bone, hot lumps of jagged metal,
Gas, smoke, fear, darkness, dissolution
By the clock, if any clock ticked on.
0940 hours: infantry attack begins,
Across the broken earth, the broken men.
An orderly advance; they sauntered
Over the unstrung landscape.

You remember your state:

Fear, fog, solitude,
Between Bullecourt and Croisilles,
Between the Staffords and the Suffolks.
We had to man the Forward Zone,
But creeping with the creeping fog
Came in the enemy. We knew them
By the shape of their helmets. They were
Where we were. Nothing was where
It had been on the map, and no one
Was one of us. The counties melted,

And their quiet local voices. My friend
Died, I was on my own.

You remember your mood:

Orphaned. The formal beauty
Of rank, its cordial courteous bearing,
Had foundered. No one to give
Or receive orders. Our training
Was scrappy; we had never studied
The delicate art of retreat, and our trumpets
Had mud in their throats.

You remember your choice:

Flight. Through craters, corpses,
Stumps of horses, guns and trees,
Through fog and my everyman darkness.
What are the rules for the solitary
Soldier? Should he stand firm
To the last pointless volley,
Or lay down his arms at the feet
Of kind enemies, and be whisked
By their finished techniques
To a snug internment? No one
Had drilled enterprise into us.
Choice had been frightened to death.
I could do only what I did,
What the primitive man I muzzle
Inside me made me do: I ran.

You remember the sequel:

Rehabilitation. The comfort of being
Among confederates, men
Who had hobbled their way back, stubbornly,
Without heroism. Most of us still
Had our uses. Mine was liaison
With American troops. Gigantic,
Buoyant, ignorant, they trod
Our shellshocked fief, as once their ancestors

Trampled across the New World.
I guided them along the labyrinths,
Interpreted, explained, a ghost of war,
Leading the living down the dead men's trenches.

You remember your self:

I had archaic longings,
Yearned for the dead and the lost,
The officers, the other ranks, the men
I belonged with, who knew the same songs,
Shouted on United. Not even
Graves for most, just Memorials
To the Missing. I missed them,
All the canny Geordie lads
With their feet still through the night
And the days.

2. SPOILS OF PEACE

Some of the dead were signallers:
Rupert the Fair and Wilfred the Wise,
Isaac the exile and innocent Ivor,
And Edward, who endured.

In various ways, these died,
And so, afterwards, in some ways,
Some of the living perhaps listened.

The dead can afford to be generous,
Having no superannuation rights.
These men squandered the spoils of war,
But I latched on to my red-edged learning,

Investing sensibly in job, house, car,
Wife and children, dog and skivvy.
Redoubts and outworks, manned by me,
To balk the enemy at my back.

I couldn't afford to be taken
The same way twice; kept short accounts,
Checked the wiring, planted sharp roses,
Trained the dog to the *qui vive*.

But upkeep has to be paid for. I traded
My craftsman's hands for a salesman's pay.
Built my house on my tongue. Charm
Was the mortar, the brickwork cheek.

In a world fit for heroes, heroism
Is *de trop*. You have to fight
With guile for your rights, against
The agenda-adept, the minutes-men.

I mastered the means that made men mine,
Not shadows, to fade in the gassed thicket,
But beefy reliable cheque-signing fingers,
Dewlaps to dance at my bagman's patter.

I held the line, from Wallsend to Workington,
Where the Romans were, I came.
Chatted up waitresses, chaffed the barmen,
Sold my soul to keep myself safe.

(Not between Croisilles and Bullecourt.)

Good morning!
           Good gracious!
                      Nice day.
                            Delightful.
Any tonics, tinctures or pick-me-ups?
No.
Thank you. I'll call again.
                      Good morning.
                            Nice day.

Where the wind whips over the fraying border,
Where homesick legions were whittled away,
On the frontier of failure I jobbed and prospered,
Natty, dapper, with my quickfire smile.

Not the dovetailed sockets, the tonguing and grooving,
The crisscross network I could have carved,
But a web of hardheaded sceptical buyers,
Whom I forced at jokepoint to be my friends.

Good morning!
            Good morning.
                        Nice day.
                                Yes.
Any false rumours, horrors or hangovers?
No thank you.
I'll call again.
            Do.
                    Good morning.
                                Good morning.
Shocking day.

Back at HQ the walls stood firm.
I saw to that. But the garrison
Could never be trusted. Maids
Came and went, children were born

And died. The dog too. I procured
Replacements, held weekly inspections,
Reviewed morale, kept up my payments,
Insured house, contents and livestock, checked

The defences. There was nothing amiss.
But somehow I had enlisted
A saboteur, not a friend (my friend
Died). She gave me nothing

To complain of; collaborated in all
Transactions, performed creditably
At trade functions, answered the telephone
Adequately. But I didn't like

The sort of book she read. Disaffection
Was plain in her children. The boy
A myopic coward, whose only solution
Was running away. Then the girl

86

Who died. I forget her name now,
But she cost me a mint of money
At the time, one way and the other.
As for the substitute, I recognized

A usurper in her. She'd have ousted
Me, taken my place if she could,
Mutinous, sulky, and damnably
Heir to my look and my hands.

I had carved out a kingdom
For my son to inherit. But he
Renegued, would have none of it,
Fancied his own improvident way,

Instead of cultivating my contacts.
Married a fatherless, unsuitable
Outspoken girl from down south somewhere,
Ran to the opposite end of the earth

And stayed there. Good riddance.
One less mouth to feed, one less craven
In the camp. The girl deserted too,
After a prolonged, costly education

Without a dividend. No hope there
Of a son-in-law, someone I could
Have trusted, canny chap, living close,
To keep an eye on the wiring, the blood-pressure,

Someone I could have taken to, without
That yellow streak in him. But I managed
Without. Anticipated the next assault
(Infirmity, loneliness, death) and took

Precautionary measures: transferred HQ
To a high-rise residence for the well-heeled,
Heated centrally, caretakered, with lift,
Where care would be taken.

Here we live now, annuitied. I ignore
The persistent trickle of offstage
Deaths, as my feebler contemporaries
Fall out. Life has taught me
To concentrate on living. This I do.

My primitive man is dead, crushed
By cordial years of cronies. I couldn't
Speak straight now if I tried.
I am the kerbside cheapjack's patter:

Ladies, watch what I do.
The genuine article. 20 pound in the catalogue,
18 in the shops, 15 in the sales. But from me –
Stand close, ladies – *a fiver*!
Ladies, watch what I do.

Watch, ladies, what I do.
Holidays abroad yearly, until age
Made us uninsurable. Now a five-star
Scottish hydro, where I am known

To the management. I am still standing to,
Between the Staffords and the Suffolks,
As I have been for most of my life.
I may be only a tin soldier,
But I have been constant.

FROM *Voices Off*

Tomorrow and

(for J. R. who reads Cowper while dying of cancer)

Was and *will be* are both uneasy ground;
Now is the safest tense.

Terminal Care rests among recipes
On the kitchen table.

We choke the future back down our throats like
Incipient vomit,

With so much time ahead, for all we know,
For turning out cupboards,

Pottery courses, Greek holidays, Brahms,
Grandchildren, greenhouses,

Getting at last to the end of *Decline
And Fall of the Roman*

It's all indifferent to him. He won't
Be here. Our small concerns

Balk us with their familiarity.
His perspectives are strict.

Library fines and income tax returns
Have lost their sting. The huge

Ghouls that shadow old age have excused him.
His exacting lover

Arrogates all of him. He'll never grow
Senile, tiresome, lonely.

With stoic courtesy, unfortified
By rites of holy church,

He watches each tomorrow, appraises
Contour, climate, colour,

As if it were a new world, while his books
(Which he won't read again,

He says) rest idle on their shelves, and nights
Grow longer, and contain

More symptoms, and his friends come, go, come, go,
Swallowing hereafters,

And he transacts the same
Miniature feats of gallantry with which
Cowper restrained the dark

Once, as far as we know

Robert Lindsay's Hamlet

(for Braham Murray)

That's him, in the foetal position, among
The front row watchers,

Sweatshirt and jeans, nothing particular, you
Wouldn't look twice, till

He stands to pace that eccentric circuit, from
Clouds still hang on you

To *Cracks a noble heart*, with the special props
That signal the Prince:

Two swords, recorders, skulls, a cup and a book.
The junk has banked up

Along the years. He can't move a foot without
Dislodging clinker –

First Folio, the good Quarto, bright guesses
From dead editors,

A notion of Goethe's, a sad hometruth of
Seedy STC's,

Business inherited from great-grandfathers
Garrick, Kean, Irving –

Heir to all this, as his watchers are heirs
Of dead playgoers,

Coming to see what they already know, with
Astonish me! smiles.

Who could mime anything new from this heap of
Old British rubbish?

But this man, discarding limelight and ketchup,
Customary suits,

Delivered raw at each performance, elbows
Us along the trite

Life of the man who thought faster than any-
one ever, till we,

Losing our poise, are lost, like the ignorant
Playgoer, watching

The story, whispering at the wrong moment
Does he kill him now?

Patients

Not the official ones, who have been
Diagnosed and made tidy. They are
The better sort of patient.

They know the answers to the difficult
Questions on the admission sheet
About religion, next of kin, sex.

They know the rules. The printed ones
In the *Guide for Patients*, about why we prefer
No smoking, the correct postal address;

Also the real ones, like the precise quota
Of servility each doctor expects,
When to have fits, and where to die.

These are not true patients. They know
Their way around, they present the right
Symptoms. But what can be done for us,

The undiagnosed? What drugs
Will help our Matron, whose cats are
Her old black husband and her young black son?

Who will prescribe for our nurses, fatally
Addicted to idleness and tea? What therapy
Will relieve our Psychiatrist of his lust

For young slim girls, who prudently
Pretend to his excitement, though age
Has freckled his hands and his breath smells old?

How to comfort our Director through his
Terminal distress, as he babbles of
Football and virility, trembling in sunlight?

There is no cure for us. O, if only
We could cherish our bizarre behaviour
With accurate clinical pity. But there are no

Notes to chart our journey, no one
Has even stamped CONFIDENTIAL or *Not to be
Taken out of the hospital* on our lives.

Man to Man

Your divers' bubbling summons has roused
Us at our mooring, where we lay
Waiting for Gabriel.

We are the men who foundered, who plunged
Smartly to our stations, under
The eyes of the bright king

In July weather, in a flat calm,
In home waters, among the fleet,
Without giving reasons.

The long wait spliced us. Artificers,
Officers, gunmen and bowmen,
Old salts, surgeons, sea-cooks,

Captain, Vice-Admiral, all of us
Lay together in our common
Catafalque like lovers.

Tides passed. The mild fish consumed our flesh,
Bones dropped neat and nice as rope coils,
Jaws fell, grinning welcome

To the certain resurrection, when
The lovely rigging of the bone
Leaps to the last whistle

Of Bo'sun Christ. But the next coming
Was yours, who harrowed our petty
Harvest of every day –

Boots, bricks, barrels, baskets, rigging-blocks,
Dice, daggers, dead-eyes, pipe-and-drum,
A bell, books, candlesticks,

Hairs of the ship's dog, bones of the rat
He might have caught, bones of the men
Embalmed in Solent mud.

What will you do with us, you to whom
The sea yields its secrets, who plumbed
Our permanent instant?

Museums will house our chattels. Even
Degraded wood has its uses.
Only our nameless bones

Remain dully unadaptable,
Impossible to show or sell,
Being the same as yours.

Growing Up

I wasn't good
At being a baby. Burrowed my way
Through the long yawn of infancy,
Masking by instinct how much I knew
Of the senior world, sabotaging
As far as I could, biding my time,
Biting my rattle, my brother (in private),
Shoplifting daintily into my pram.
Not a good baby,
No.

I wasn't good
At being a child. I missed
The innocent age. Children,
Being childish, were beneath me.
Adults I despised or distrusted. They
Would label my every disclosure
Precocious, *naïve*, whatever it was.
I disdained definition, preferred to be surly.
Not a nice child,
No.

I wasn't good
At adolescence. There was a dance,
A catchy rhythm; I was out of step.
My body capered, nudging me
With hairy, fleshy growths and monthly outbursts,
To join the party. I tried to annul
The future, pretended I knew it already,
Was caught bloody-thighed, a criminal
Guilty of puberty.
Not a nice girl,
No.

(My hero, intransigent Emily,
Cauterized her own-dog-mauled
Arm with a poker,
Struggled to die on her feet,
Never told anyone anything.)

I wasn't good
At growing up. Never learned
The natives' art of life. Conversation
Disintegrated as I touched it,
So I played mute, wormed along years,
Reciting the hard-learned arcane litany
Of cliché, my company passport.
Not a nice person,
No.

The gift remains
Masonic, dark. But age affords
A vocation even for wallflowers.
Called to be connoisseur, I collect,
Admire, the effortless bravura
Of other people's lives, proper and comely,
Treading the measure, shopping, chaffing,
Quarrelling, drinking, not knowing
How right they are, or how, like well-oiled bolts,
Swiftly and sweet, they slot into the grooves
Their ancestors smoothed out along the grain.

Weather Map

The island, from Wight to Wrath,
Thumbed blank as innocence.

All that is left, the faithless
Unfailing sea, common land
Of the winds. Nobody left
To register tides, compute gale force,
Read and transmit clouds' delicate
Incessant early warning.

The winds will wander, unwatched, unremarked,
Down parishes we nodded at, cosily,
After the News, before the new world.
Fuming along their provinces they go,
Fair Isle and Forties,
Dogger, Bight, Humber,
Thames, Dover, Portland,
Sole, Finisterre.

And not a hair to float upon the breeze.

London Z to A

Her buildings come and go like leaves.
Ziggurats bud. New highways soar
Like suckers, ambitious into air.

Behind the boarded windows
Pruning happens.

In the marble city only the barbarous
Street names last.

And driving south
Down remembered gone roads, the cheesy
Cockney faces blossom in witty
Brittle façades: *Stark Naked
Ltd*; *A Touch of Glass*; *Den
Of Antiquity*; *Just Looking*; *Just 4 U*;
Hat Trick. The strictly dapper parks
Offer no comment. But the corner pubs
Honour forgotten generals, dispossessed peers,
A stag, a tree; and streaming rude
Over tarmac and paving, barks, bellows, halloos,
Men, dogs and cattle, Lewisham awash
With their steaming muddy passage,
The Kentish Drovers.

Circus Tricks

Clearly Eden. Figleaves are out,
But they wear their meticulous muscles
As casually as clothes. They can fly,
And do, briefly, to a thrumming rumble,
Silence, a major chord on brass.

They rule matter. Plates and skittles
Duck humbly to their palms, and bunting
Interminably issues from their elbows;
They gyrate on an ear, an unambitious bone.

Obliging creatures, rash with love,
Unselve themselves, and do the splits to please.
A seal flops after Eve; Adam lays
His head in the tiger's tolerant nutcracker chops;
Emeritus apes play silly monkey-tricks;
Elephants amble hand-in-hand; barbs bow
Their lovelocked heads; dogs bear the foolish ruff.

The whip is ornament. It merely points.
Nobody here gets hurt, except the child,
Artless in Eden, who assumes
All this is natural, the worried dullness
Of household pets, the sagging clothbound bodies
Of Mum and Dad just a mistake.

The Windsors: An Everyday Story of Royal Folk

Some people honestly believe in them,
Think they're alive, write to them, send them flowers,
Are always knitting for the newest one,
Keep albums crammed with snaps of what they've done,
Wave flags in rainswept streets for hours and hours,
    With a Grundy here and a Gloucester there,
        Here a chukka, there a chicken, here and there a corgi.
            Mrs Windsor has a realm;
            God save gracious Dan!

Some people need another family
A touch more charismatic than their own,
Glossy at Goodwood, funny at a fête,
Sound with a tractor or the Ship of State,
Despite zoom lenses goggling at their throne,
    At Prince Andrew, Shula Archer, Mrs Simpson, Mrs Perkins,
        Walter Gabriel, Princess Di,
        Old Uncle Tom Forrest and all,
        Great-uncle Mountbatten and all.

Their history is ours; our parents knew
The small print of their genealogy.
They're loyal to their fans; they seldom stray;
Death changes the cast-list, but not the play,
And when we turn the switch on, there they'll be
    Doing their bit
        for
        Garter King of Arms
        BBC
        And the NFU
        With a crown in the family tree.

'Soothing and Awful'

(Visitors' Book at Montacute church)

You are meant to exclaim. The church
Expects it of you. Bedding plants
And polished brass anticipate a word.

Visitors jot a name,
A nationality, briskly enough,
But find *Remarks* beyond them.

I love English churches!
Says Friedrichshafen expansively.
The English are more backward. They come,

Certainly, from Spalding, Westbury-on-Trym,
The Isle of Wight; but all the words
They know are: *Very Lovely*; *Very Peaceful*; *Nice*.

A giggling gaggle from Torquay Grammar,
All pretending they can't spell *beautiful*, concoct
A private joke about the invisible organ.

A civilized voice from Cambridge
Especially noticed the well-kept churchyard.
Someone from Dudley, whose writing suggests tight shoes,

Reported *Nice and Cool*. The young entry
Yelp their staccato approval:
Super! Fantastic! Jesus Lives! Ace!

But what they found,
Whatever it was, it wasn't what
They say. In the beginning,

We know, the word, but not here,
Land of the perpetually-flowering cliché,
The rigid lip. Our fathers who piled

Stone upon stone, our mothers
Who stitched the hassocks, our cousins
Whose bones lie smooth, harmonious around –

However majestic their gifts, comely their living,
Their words would be thin like ours; they would join
In our inarticulate anthem: *Very Cosy*.

Purton Lower Bridge

Affable water lips and chats
Along iron-bound banks. A cruiser's wake
Wags unendingly after it, floats flouncing
Like cross dowagers with long memories.
Not many boats in autumn. Boys
Lend a hand with ropes, show their catch
(A dead eel). The low swung bridge
Opens when needed, smoothly, like a sliced smile.

This is the human scale: nothing too much.
But half a mile downstream sprawls Glumdalclitch,
Naked, enormous, careless, bright with mud,
Red sun squat on her, pocked by birdfeet, cables,
Monstrously tidal, impossible, uncivil,
Desirable, the lethal river Severn.

The First Years Arrive

You could mistake it for a holiday.
Rucksacks around, and dormobiles,
And people running to and fro with bundles.
But no one eats. That comes later

And is significant. They will eat
When the crowd has gone, with the new
Uncertain friends. But still you could
Mistake it for a holiday. There are

Grans sitting on beds, and younger sisters
On windowsills; the dog walks up
And down outside on a lead.
And no one cries. That is significant

And came earlier. *We're past*
The worst moment says a mother wryly.
Hers will be later, when she moves
An un-needed chair away from the breakfast table.

Fathers dashingly shoulder trunks upstairs,
Feeling their age. But you could still mistake.
They aim at a bright surface. No one
Cuddles in public. That comes later

And is significant. The time to go.
Misery keeps to itself. In one room three
Keep the door closed, and mother
Has taken her shoes off. Grief

Is not taken on holiday, or qualms.
The new uncertain friends, the well-used walls,
Even the virginal files, may hold more learning
Of false notes than is practised at home.

But that comes later, a holiday away,
Beyond the sphere of grans and younger sisters,
When, families gone, they have eaten and drunk,
And each lamb's left alone in the well-used thicket.

Being a Student

(Fourth week, First Year)

Unless you become the eternal kind
It lasts three years; time
To get married, divorced,
Re-married, or for Christ's ministry.

Standing-water time. Time
So much wanted that
When it comes, you can't believe
That it's here. Am I truly

That godlike thing? Do junior
School kids, seeing me, think
Student, the way they recognize
A blackbird, the way I did?

The feeling hasn't arrived yet.
Inside I'm still last year's
Sixth-former, pretending. At home they'd see
Through my jeans and leg-warmers

To the uniform self, caged
Between O and A. Here I'm defined
By last year's crop. The cleaner
Thinks I'll turn out like the girl

Who had this room before. *Easy
Meat!* she says, and sucks
Her cheeks, investigating the wastepaper
Basket for signs of sin.

My spelling mistakes are old
Friends to my new tutor. He keeps
Calling me *Mandy*, too. He sees
Three or four of me, cloudily.

And all the time the great
Term revolves, like the gerbils'
Wheel at home, and light falls
In unique patterns each day

On the sea and the fell,
And none of it comes again ever,
So rich, so wild, so fast,
While inside me I haven't

Even arrived here yet.

The Cleaner

I've seen it all, you know. Men.
Well, I've been married for thirty-two years,
I can do without them.
I know what they're after.

And these students. They're young, you know.
They don't know what it's all about,
The first years. And these post-grads;
I know what they're after.

They're older, you know. And by Christmas
They've finished here, they've gone. A girl
Can get hurt. I've been here eight years.
I've seen it happen.

Sometimes I say to her friend
*You ought to talk to her. Does she know
What she's doing?* And the friend'll say
Yes, she does know. Well, I hope I did right.

No need for any of 'em to have a baby,
But do they know? I feel a mother, like.
Once I did ask. I said *Do you know*
And she said *O yes, we know how far we're going.*

But these post-grads are older,
They take advantage. These girls, mind,
They're not all as innocent as you'd think.
Twenty stubs in the ashtray.

I can tell a lot from that.

Knowing about Sonnets

Lesson 1: 'The Soldier' (Brooke)

'[The task of criticism] is not to redouble the text's self-understanding, to collude with its object in a conspiracy of silence. The task is to show the text as it cannot know itself.'

Terry Eagleton, *Criticism and Ideology*

Recognizing a sonnet is like attaching
A name to a face. *Mister Sonnet, I presume?*
    If I
And naming is power. It can hardly
Deny its name. You are well on the way
To mastery. The next step is telling the sonnet
What it is trying to say. This is called Interpretation.
    If I should die
What you mustn't do is collude with it. This
Is bad for the sonnet, and will only encourage it
To be eloquent. You must question it closely:
What has it left out? What made it decide
To be a sonnet? The author's testimony
(If any) is not evidence. He is the last person to know.
    If I should die, think this
Stand no nonsense with imagery. Remember, though shifty,
It is vulnerable to calculation. Apply the right tests.
Now you are able to Evaluate the sonnet.
    If I
That should do for today.
    If I should die
               And over and over
The new white paper track innocent unlined hands.
    Think this. Think this. Think this. Think only this.

Seminar: Felicity and Mr Frost

(*for Helen and Felicity Clark*)

Two truth-tellers are here;
Marigold-headed Felicity (three)
Has come because of a hole in the roof.
Mr Frost, who is dead, comes in black
On white. He has something to tell us.

Both try hard. Felicity
Has drawn a house, silent
As thinking. *Can we have a door?*
She whispers. Mr Frost has brought a wall

With holes in it. The holes grow
Larger and darker as the sun
Walks round the room. Felicity
Opens her mouth in a yawn like a hole.

*I didn't understand the story
The man was telling us* she says clearly
Underneath the table. Mr Frost
Sticks to his story, but his voice is opaque.

After a cuddle, a thumb-suck, Felicity
Touches the book with her hand,
Gravely. It is snowing now in Mr Frost.
He has written a very short poem

And Felicity has found a jimmy in it
(*Secret world*, her mother explains).
Mr Frost's world is secret too.
There are woods in it, and miles to go,

And snow. It has started to rain
Where we are. Felicity stands on a chair
To look out. *Don't ever have children*,
Her mother smiles at the students.

And miles to go. *You said*
Don't have children (Felicity cancels
Her secret world). The students are concerned.
It is still raining. Her mother translates:

I didn't mean it. And snowing.
Mr Frost is preoccupied. He
Has promises to keep. And miles to go.

Dig

The place: once Troy; the characters:
Ghosts of two Trojan lovers who lived there;

The time: a dream of mine; the plot:
Nothing . . . driftings and strayings round a spot

That neither recognized. Where were
The god-built walls, the gates, the bright river?

A wind got up: the famous wind.
The sad ghosts sighed and drifted like dry sand.

Only an archaeologist
Could disinter what these cold phantoms missed:

Village on top of village; town
On town; city on city; Trojan ground

Lay aeons under Hissarlik.
Schliemann alone could recognize the wreck

And spell it Ilium; he who
Unpicked the wayward river's fluent clew,

Found the old bed of Scamander
Far from Mendere's prosy meander.

My dream-ghosts never traced their Troy.
In waking life, dear lost one, you and I

Whose Troy fell centuries ago
Find, when we meet, the malign debris grow:

Misunderstandings; blunders; slips;
Faults; different lives that have developed since.

Useless to salvage what has been.
At once the monstrous midden sprouts between.

Chaplaincy Fell Walk

There is always one out in front
With superior calves and experienced boots;

Always a final pair to be waited for,
Not saying much, pale, rather fat;

And the holy ones in the middle, making it
Their part to acclimatize the lonely and new,
Introducing cinquefoil, a heron, a view;

And a stout one who giggles, uniting us
In wonder at her unfaltering chokes;
But alarming too. For what is she laughing at?

And remote presence of hills;
And the absence of you.

The Sheepdog

After the very bright light,
And the talking bird,
And the singing,
And the sky filled up wi' wings,
And then the silence,

Our lads sez
We'd better go, then.
Stay, Shep. Good dog, stay.
So I stayed wi' t' sheep.

After they cum back,
It sounded grand, what they'd seen:
Camels, and kings, and such,
Wi' presents – human sort,
Not the kind you eat –
And a baby. Presents wes for him.
Our lads took him a lamb.

I had to stay behind wi' t' sheep.
Pity they didn't tek me along too.
I'm good wi' lambs,
And the baby might have liked a dog
After all that myrrh and such.

The Person's Tale

'In consequence of a slight indisposition, an anodyne had been prescribed, from the effects of which [the author] fell asleep . . . On awaking . . . [he] eagerly wrote down the lines that are here preserved. At this moment he was unfortunately called out by a person on business from Porlock, and detained by him above an hour . . .'

S. T. C.

That the Muses have no more fervent
Devotee than myself may not be generally
Known outside Porlock. As a man of the cloth
I am, I trust, superior to mere vulgar
Appetite for fame. 'Full many a gem
Of purest ray serene . . .' I am, I hope, resigned
To being such a gem; an unseen blush.
But to allow myself to be presented
By Mr C— to posterity as a *person*
Goes beyond the limits of even clerical
Diffidence. It was, I may say, in pursuit
Of my pastoral duties that I made
The not inconsiderable journey from my parsonage
To the farmhouse, at Mr C—'s own
Most vehement behest. Prepared for any
Extreme office, I presented myself
Before Mr C—, *Sir*, said I, *I am here.*
The very man, quoth he, clasping me in
A distasteful embrace. *Most reverend sir –*
Then for two hours detained me at his door
With chronicles of colic, stomach, bowels,
Of nightly sweats, the nightmare, cramps, diarrhoea
(Your pardon, Delicacy! Merely the word appals),
All the while straining me to his bosom, like
His own deplorable Mariner, neglected hygiene
Rendering contiguity less than welcome,
The more as I infallibly discerned

The less pleasing features of addiction
To the poppy, prescribed, he affirmed,
As anodyne against the dysentery.
And now, it seems, I am the guilty *person*
Who cut off inspiration in its prime.
Quite otherwise. Myself had on the way
Entertained the notion of an Acrostick, a form
Of harmless mirth whereby I have achieved
Some slender fame among the Porlock fair.
Alas! the frail thing could not survive
Two hours of Mr C—'s internal ills.
I am the loser, first of my Acrostick,
Then of my character, for surely *person*
Denotes nonentity, a man of straw –
And the proud name of Porlock sullied too!

Local Poet

Can't see so well now; his hearing
Isn't what it was. But he can still
Smell where a fox has been among the dahlias.

The birds have flown, the loft's empty,
But he still writes for *Pigeon Post*,
Plays cards with his ancient neighbour,

Works the garden. And suddenly,
A year ago, the Muse pounced:
He is her man in Gloucestershire.

The opposition doesn't worry him. *Betjeman, now –*
He rhymes too far apart. I have 'em close
Like church bells. I'm ready for publication.

Each poem's numbered like a show bird;
There's a prospectus: 'Purchasers will find them
Humorous, informative, historical.'

And so they will, they will. The W.I.
Like his stuff; and the Horticultural.
His voice helps. Double Gloucester,

Though it shouldn't be, he says. *I had the best*
Education available at that time.
But I liked to play with the wild boys,

And they spoke broad. Now he's the poet
For wild things, looks with a pigeon's eye
As far north as Evesham, tells how blackbirds

Lob home though ivy, where to find
The fishbone mixen of a kingfisher's nest,
Honours the useful stream by the elastic factory,

Explains how to direct hounds (*they know
Who Charlie is*), records shy Royalty's local earths,
The tragedy of the lame stray greyhound bitch

Whose litter the fox ate, gulls
Trailing wireworms down strict furrows,
Long-dead shires with hooves

As big as buckets, and remembers
Ol' Tucker Workman trapping the badger
Using his legs like tongs. But most of all

I like his garden ones, about the flowers
He grows but cannot spell, bees feverish
For marrow pollen, the evening mating call

Of woodlice, his iambic prescription
For limp cauliflowers of calomel dust
(*Obtainable from Boots*). How can I tell him

The competition judge won't pick his poems?
The Horticultural, the W.I. –
They ask him back, they think he's good,

And they know what he's on about. *This judge –
Where's he from, anyway? He won't know here.*
We settle which to send. He's disappointed

By what I like. I know he has no chance
Of winning. Does he trust me? No, I think.
Can he suspect I'll write about our talk,

And steal all his best lines? I hope he can't.
I hope he won't read this.

Women Laughing

Gurgles, genderless,
Inside the incurious womb.

Random soliloquies of babies
Tickled by everything.

Undomesticated shrieks
Of small girls. Mother prophesies
You'll be crying in a minute.

Adolescents wearing giggles
Like chain-mail, against embarrassment,
Giggles formal in shape as
Butterpats, or dropped stitches.

Young women anxious to please,
Laughing eagerly before the punchline
(Being too naïve to know which it is).

Wives gleaming sleekly in public at
Husbandly jokes, masking
All trace of old acquaintance.

Mums obliging with rhetorical
Guffaws at the children's riddles
That bored their parents.

Old women, unmanned, free
Of children, embarrassment, desire to please,
Hooting grossly, without explanation.

From the Third Storey

(*for Hazel Medd*)

'You have to be selfish to be a writer.'
'Monstrously selfish?'
'Monstrously selfish,' she said.
   Jean Rhys in David Plante's *Difficult Women*

Aunt Jane scribbles in the living-room.
When visitors come, she stuffs her work
Under the blotter, and joins in the chat.

(In the third storey, a curious
Laugh; distinct, formal, mirthless.)

Daughter Charlotte's first care is to discharge
Her household and filial duties. Only then
May she admit herself to her own bright sphere.

(There were days when she was quite silent;
Others when I could not account for
The sounds she made.)

Home duties are a small part of
The Reverend William's life. Reverently
Elizabeth, wife and mother, furnishes his study,
And writes in the dining-room,
Which has three doors.

(A vague murmur, peculiar
And lugubrious. Something
Gurgled and moaned.)

George is Agnes's husband. He and
Mistress Marian (*what do people call her?*)
Write in one room at their desks, drudging
To pay off his marriage's debts.

(A savage, a sharp, a shrilly sound.
The thing delivering such utterance must rest
Ere it repeat the effort. It came
Out of the third storey.)

Sister Virginia, childless wife,
Fathoms the metaphor of room.
But who is One? The upstairs lunatic –
Might she not be Oneself?

(A snarling, snatching sound,
Almost like a dog quarrelling.)

Between affairs, before marriages,
Jean (*I have called myself so many
Different names*) buys twelve technicoloured
Quill pens to cheer her bare table
In bedsit Fulham. And writes,

(She was standing, waving her arms,
Above the battlements, and shouting out
Till they could hear her a mile off.)

And sets the mad wife free to tell
Truth of mistress, divorcée, mother,
Aunt, daughter, sister, wife:

*Now at last I know
Why I was brought here
And what I have to do.*

READ MORE IN PENGUIN

READ MORE IN PENGUIN

A SELECTION OF POETRY

American Verse
British Poetry since 1945
Caribbean Verse in English
Chinese Love Poetry
A Choice of Comic and Curious Verse
Contemporary American Poetry
Contemporary British Poetry
Contemporary Irish Poetry
English Poetry 1918–60
English Romantic Verse
English Verse
First World War Poetry
German Verse
Greek Verse
Homosexual Verse
Imagist Poetry
Irish Verse
Japanese Verse
The Metaphysical Poets
Modern African Poetry
New Poetry
Poetry of the Thirties
Scottish Verse
Surrealist Poetry in English
Spanish Verse
Victorian Verse
Women Poets
Zen Poetry